W9-BIP-439

WITHDRAWN

UNIVERSITY OF MINNESOTA

Harold Frederic

BY STANTON GARNER

UNIVERSITY OF MINNESOTA PRESS · MINNEAPOLIS

Printed in the United States of America at
the North Central Publishing Company, St. Paul

Library of Congress Catalog Card Number: 73-628286

PUBLISHED IN GREAT BRITAIN, INDIA, AND PAKISTAN BY THE OXFORD
UNIVERSITY PRESS, LONDON, BOMBAY, AND KARACHI, AND IN CANADA
BY THE COPP CLARK PUBLISHING CO. LIMITED, TORONTO

HAROLD FREDERIC

STANTON GARNER, an associate professor of English at Brown University, is working on a full-length study of Harold Frederic and collaborating in the preparation of a volume of the collected letters of Frederic.

↗ Harold Frederic

In early 1883, Harold Frederic wrote a eulogy to a young poet who had died before the promise of his career could be fulfilled. At the time he was preoccupied with thoughts of fame which might transcend death. "Worse than the terrors of dissolution itself is the fear that death may bring forgetfulness. The oldest graven records of the race are barriers raised to stop this dread oblivion, — at once a protest against the effacing march of generations and a plea for posterity's attention, pitiful in its helplessness. 'Let his name be forgotten,' was the sternest and most merciless form of ancient condemnation." Though referring to another, the words, written at a time when Frederic himself was preparing for a literary career, say far more about the novelist than about the forgotten poet.

For Frederic was ambitious to earn a place among the greatest of those whose names were recorded in the "graven records of the race." And, judging from the evidence then available to him, there was every reason to anticipate that he would. Only twenty-six years old, he was already a successful newspaper editor for the second time. A brilliant, articulate, forceful man, he had served apprenticeships as a novice painter and as an author of modest but publishable short stories, and had in progress a novel which, he hoped, would bring him fame. As an editor, he had already influenced a significant segment of New York State political opinion and been instrumental in the election of Grover Cleveland as governor. Many well-remembered men had done far less at Frederic's age.

Nor did he fail to realize much of his promise. As a journalist,

5

he has been given much of the credit for developing the *New York Times* into an international newspaper. His columns were distinguished by aggressive reporting and luminous insight into events. Most important, he succeeded in fulfilling much of his potential as a literary artist. After a painful trial period, he produced a small body of distinguished novels and novellas, one of which ranks very high among American works of the century. Yet in fifteen years he was dead, and soon thereafter his name was forgotten with that of the poet he eulogized, his works scarcely read, and it is only in recent years that scholars have revived interest in him and made tentative beginnings toward an evaluation of his achievement. Surely literary fortune has rarely rebuffed so summarily a man who, with good reason, expected so much of it.

Harold Frederic committed himself to a literary career in 1874. It was mid-June when he sailed from New York City to London aboard the steamer *Queen* as London correspondent of the *New York Times*, and thus became a member of that earlier, more innocent pre-Hemingway wave of American expatriates who crossed the Atlantic, not to escape America, but to rediscover Europe. Frederic was not a runaway, but a confident American in the tradition of Ralph Waldo Emerson and Walt Whitman, optimistic, self-reliant, burly, robust, democratic. From Whitman and Emerson, and more remotely Ben Franklin, he had inherited a typically American understanding of the nature of reality: that the universe proceeds according to a dependable cosmic timetable along an undeviating track, leading not to Hawthorne's chill waters but to a secular Celestial City filled with gawdy rewards for the diligent whose actions harmonize with that order. Accordingly, the freedom and unlimited opportunity of America permit the vigorous to rise according to their merit and industry to eminence. Rising from poverty to affluence, discovering the nature of lightning, writing a great book widely read and applauded, all these result from the same harmony with the spheres. Like many another American of his time, though more tentatively, Frederic accepted this as a working principle of life.

Yet Frederic was not without Hawthorne-like doubts. There had been moments of disharmony in his life when the principle had failed, when with the best of intentions he had mistaken the main chance, and certain self-destructive temptations had proved irresistible — to his disgust. He was after all not formed in an amiable Unitarian tradition, like Emerson, or in an atmosphere of Quaker calm and light, like Whitman, but in the sterner Methodist discipline. Unlike them, he retained an intuitive sense of the sinfulness of man's nature, although he rejected sin conceptually. Furthermore, as a young reporter along the Erie Canal he had witnessed scenes of cruelty and degradation for which his democratic idealism failed to account.

Because of this ambivalence in Frederic's personality, close acquaintances often erred seriously in estimating his qualities. They saw his veneer of rough force, heard his quick repartee and tireless joviality. But they failed to see the complex mind, the depth of introspection, and the refinement of sensibility beneath; it was from this deeper level of apprehension that fiction of lasting importance eventually came.

But when he left for England he had as yet written no significant fiction. His juvenile stories were slight inventions, about a starving waif rescued from the snow by a rich man who proves to be her father, about a girl disguised as a monk in a French monastery, and about symbolic brothers with opposing loyalties in the American Revolution. His present ambitions were far grander. For seven years he had worked fitfully on a historical romance of the Revolutionary period, and saw in the independence of his life in England an opportunity to complete it. In addition, he had half-formed plans for a trilogy of novels of contemporary upstate New York, patterned after Disraeli's Young England novels and beginning, as in *Coningsby*, with a study of American politics.

He envisioned a far different return to America. "I dream," he had written, "of the day when I can command a living by honest work in good humane literature, as the anchorite dreams of the day when he shall exchange his hair-shirt for the white robe." Two or three years of work and the white robe would be his, and he could cast aside the hair shirt of journalism. He would then return triumphantly to America to take his place on Parnassus with Emerson, Hawthorne, and Howells. Much later, when his dreams of immediate success had proved overly sanguine, he could still write, "I'm not a Hawthorne, but as the small Charleston darkey said to the old one, who insisted on God's superiority over the black Congressman from the Sixth District — 'Yes, but don' you fohget — Bob Smalls he young man yet!' "

Frederic was born on August 19, 1856, in the Mohawk Valley city of Utica, New York. Left a widow when her son was only eighteen months old, his mother assumed the roles of both parents. Even after her remarriage, the family remained a matriarchy. It was "Frank" the woman-man who superintended the family enterprises, who dominated her home and set its tone in egalitarian politics and fundamentalist religion. She came to symbolize for Frederic the plain-featured, sturdy pioneer women of America, and as such she frequently appears thinly disguised in his works — in which there are seldom fathers.

A lively, sensitive boy, Frederic received the usual limited education of his modest circumstances. He had a natural talent for pencil sketching and scribbling stories and poems, and after his schooling was completed he experimented with the freedom of an artist's life, traveling to Boston to paint and write. For a brief

8

time in 1873 he lived irregularly with a pack of bohemian starve-lings, then found regular work as a photo retoucher. The pay was good, and he was enabled to satisfy his love of books and dandi-fied clothes. Undoubtedly, his ambitions were stimulated by Boston. The schoolroom poets and decaying Brahmins were nearby, and he read the "classic" English authors there. Perhaps because of this inspiration he decided that his future lay in writing rather than painting, and in 1875 he returned to Utica.

There Frederic set about his new career energetically, joining the staff of the Utica *Observer*, and before long the *Observer* was publishing his stories. However, he concentrated on his journalis-tic duties rather than fiction. He performed most of the routine tasks of the editorial loft, gathering daily news and reviewing traveling art exhibits and road company performances. Success, personal and professional, came fast; by 1880, just twenty-four years old, he was married, a father, managing editor of the *Ob-server*, and *enfant terrible* of Utica. All social doors were open to him, and he shared the confidences of nationally influential men. He was particularly attracted to the Irish Catholic community and its good-natured men and beautiful women. Among them he met Edward A. Terry, a priest who was for the rest of Frederic's life his closest and most faithful friend. Terry was a brilliant the-ologian whose liberal views antagonized more dogmatic Catholic clerics, and as result he was banished to the diocesan headquar-ters in Albany. After a short interval, Frederic followed him.

In 1882 the young editor was sought out to revivify the ailing Albany *Evening Journal*, an influential Republican newspaper. He told the owners that despite his former Democratic allegiance he had become an independent with Republican leanings. Truth or not, he was hired and, leaving his family in Utica, moved into bachelor quarters with Father Terry. Then in the 1882 campaign for the governorship he threw the support of the *Journal* behind the Democratic nominee, Grover Cleveland. He thereby became an intimate of Cleveland, and soon the *Journal*'s columns were demanding Cleveland for president. Frederic was a resourceful editor who stimulated the wilting paper to new life, but after it was purchased by a more scrupulous Republican in 1884 Frederic resigned rather than support the high-tariff policy of the new owner.

Was Frederic the victim of a political purge by the new owner? Or was his resignation motivated by other reasons, his growing discontent with journalism and his impatience with the tempo of his rise in the world? There is some evidence of journalistic suicide. For one thing, the complimentary publicity resulting from his resignation brought offers of important editorships. He refused them, as well as Cleveland's suggestion that he enter politics, and accepted the subordinate *Times* position in London instead. Also, not long before he resigned he had described journalism as a "vile and hollow fool-rink," and the journalist as a "fakir." Finally, he made it abundantly clear in letter after letter from London that he regarded the *Times* post as no more than a temporary haven which he intended to abandon after a year or two. It appears therefore that he left his editorial career purposefully and with some relief. Certainly the *Times* position was ideal for a restless young man of affairs who had survived the rough-and-tumble of American public life and was ready to challenge Europe, to analyze and probe it, and add it to his growing store of world knowledge.

This was the Harold Frederic who, armed with charm, wit, energy, and a handsome introductory letter from Cleveland, disembarked from the *Queen* in England in mid-1884. He moved rapidly to establish himself in London. He infiltrated the city's club world, where the news and news makers were to be found. The bohemian Savage Club and the politically important National

Liberal Club were restricted to an exclusive membership, but Cleveland's letter opened the forbidding doors easily. Soon he was intimate with many of the most influential men in England, at ease with Parliamentarians, with periodical publishers, and in the parlors, the studios, and the theaters of London.

He had also to establish a reputation as an international journalist. Immediately after his arrival, a cholera epidemic infected southern Europe, slaughtering thousands and terrifying the entire Western world. Alone among European correspondents, he visited the area and cabled a clearheaded analysis of the causes of the plague, reassuring his readers that communities which took ordinary sanitary precautions would be in no danger. His dispatches were widely reprinted, his heroism extravagantly praised, and with this single adventure his reputation as a correspondent was secured.

In politics he championed Irish home rule. He met T. P. O'Connor, Tim Healy, and Charles Stewart Parnell soon after his arrival in England, and for a number of years he was on dining and conspiratorial terms with all three. Gradually he became personally involved with the cause of Irish independence, touring the island and absorbing its customs, history, and geography. His cables became increasingly pro-Irish and he published as his own an essay which was in fact a disguised statement of policy written by the Irish leaders. By 1886 he was acting as their envoy; on a visit to America he presented the Utica Irish with a scroll signed by the Irish members of Parliament and delivered a stirring oration about the imminence of a home-rule victory.

At the time of this visit, two years of Frederic's expatriation had passed and his success had continued uninterrupted. Preeminence and fortune seemed within reach. One great desire had been fulfilled already, the birth of his first son and namesake who, he said, "represents all my hopes and aspirations." Now a second was fulfilled, a leisurely, sentimental journey to Washington with Father Terry for an intimate White House dinner with Cleveland and his new bride. And a third, literary prominence, was in sight. He had sold the first novel of his trilogy, which, Scribner's informed him, was a remarkably strong performance. Already he was at work on a stage adaptation. The Revolutionary War romance was nearly finished, needing only "pointing up" to become the American *Henry Esmond*, and Frederic confided to friends that he intended to spend no more than one additional year in Europe. Just before the sale of the novel he had asked Cleveland for the new post of consular inspector for Great Britain. But now his future seemed assured, and neither the *Times* position nor a foreign service appointment would be needed. As he banqueted with his friends in the presidential mansion he felt confident that his term in journalism was nearly at an end, and that he had arrived at the beginning of a great career in "good, humane literature."

During these first years in England, Frederic was also searching for a usable aesthetic technique. He realized that his earlier sentimentalism was inadequate to his present intentions, and that more useful literary tools were needed. His impulses had by now become strongly didactic. His years as an editor, as a confidant of reform politicians, such as Cleveland and Theodore Roosevelt, and more recently as a co-conspirator of the Irish, had encouraged a conception of fiction as an instrument for political and sociological polemic. The Victorian novelists and his native American predecessors failed to provide him with models for this purpose. The witty, formally rhetorical prose structures and the characters and situations related to the comedy of manners of the former, and the brooding darkness of the latter, were equally unsuited to the ambience of Gilded Age expansiveness and Zolaesque scientific empiricism.

Although he was a natural raconteur, Frederic was at this time wholly incapable of devising aesthetic principles of his own. Largely self-educated in the course of a busy public life, he had no critical apparatus or vocabulary. He thought in terms of accidentals rather than essentials: sufficient room in which to "turn around," the truth or mendacity of incident, and marketability. For his philosophy of fiction, he turned to the principles of realism articulated by William Dean Howells. These included the utmost fidelity to the actual scenes, actions, and language of everyday life, and the "dramatic method" of plotting, in which "real" people are set at liberty in a "real" environment to work out "real" problems without authorial interference. Optimistic assumptions underlay this method. Granted a benign cosmic order, a plot so produced should conform to an essentially comic pattern by demonstrating in its inevitable resolution the potential of the unfettered democratic man to rise to new degrees of human achievement and happiness in the American Eden. Yet Frederic also groped instinctively for a means of expressing the more complex suspicions and perceptions which could not be wholly suppressed by his Emersonian assumptions. From the first, his discipleship to Howells was qualified by the knowledge that there were disruptive elements in American life as well as those "smiling" aspects which Howells insisted upon.

"The Editor and the Schoolma'am" (1888), part short story and part essay, throws some light on his confusion. A young, vain editor of a city newspaper quarrels with a pretty schoolteacher over an essay she has submitted on "The True Place of Milton among the English Poets." His knowledge of Milton is scant, but he nevertheless arrogantly advises her to abandon such abstract themes (Frederic himself had written comparable essays). Read Dostoevski's *Crime and Punishment*, he tells her, and write "articles" from real life on "the butcher, the baker, the candlestick maker." After reading the novel she concludes, like Howells, that a vicious murder is foreign to the placid realities of America. The subdued editor protests that there is an element of violence in the American character, only to be answered with the feminine argument that "there oughtn't to be." The two marry, leaving the central question undecided. The equally matched characters speak for the two elements of Frederic's uncertainty; he is both the doubter and the doubt.

In spite of this ambivalence, Frederic had for the time sufficient faith to write two novels in the Howells mode. But his duplicity of attitude mars his otherwise strong first novel, *Seth's Brother's Wife* (1887), and its sequel. Both are set in a fictitious congressional district of upstate New York, a re-creation of his Mohawk Valley home. As in Faulkner's Yoknapatawpha County, the area contains cities and towns, individuals and families, which reappear from work to work. An entire community is created in which Frederic tests his attitudes toward American life, and, ultimately, toward the human condition.

Seth appears to be conceived as a kind of fictionalized newspaper editorial, an attempt, in the words of Thomas F. O'Donnell and Hoyt C. Franchere, to "demonstrate, in a tone of restrained optimism, that in spite of a certain drabness and apparent moral and spiritual laxity of life in upstate New York, the region could still produce from its own citizenry honest and devoted leaders who were capable of arousing the moral vigor of the public when such vigor was needed." The main concerns are journalistic: the decay of New York State agriculture under the pressure of competition from the midwestern granaries, the operation and influence of a regional newspaper, and the power structure of a district political caucus. Frederic's style is similarly journalistic. Though tinged with Addisonian rhetoric, it is essentially colloquial and descriptive, substituting for elegance and wit a muscular, often crude prose. To readers who preferred the former, it appeared that Frederic was the victim of "journalistic standards." Yet his painter's eye, his reporter's knack of getting directly to the point, and his raconteur's ability to create striking vignettes give vividness and pungency to his first novel.

The three principal concerns intersect in Seth Fairchild. Seth is threatened with a life of ignorance and despair on the ramshackle and dismembered Fairchild farm; he gains, almost loses, and then prospers in a newspaper career; and he opposes his brother Albert's cynical scheme to seize the district congressional nomination by bribery. Had Frederic had less insight into the weaknesses of men, had he not tested Seth's responses against suspicions about his own character, *Seth* might have gained in coherence while losing in significance and interest. But Frederic was unwilling to grant his protagonist the unqualified virtue which his heroic role demands.

Much of the vigor of the novel comes from its autobiographical nature; characters, incidents, and scenes are flooded with vitality as they emerge from Frederic's memory. Seth becomes Frederic's surrogate, reliving the author's youthful experiences in editorial offices and in the caucus. Even Seth's marriage to Annie Warren, arranged at the bedside of Annie's dying mother, is a re-enactment of Frederic's courtship.

But as his surrogate, Seth bears the consequences of Frederic's deep-rooted sense of insufficiency and guilt. His dissipation nearly ruins his newspaper career, and his sexual irresponsibility very nearly results in adultery with Albert's flirtatious wife Isabel. Nor is he able to conquer either of these weaknesses through self-correction. His waning journalistic fortunes are rescued at the last minute by the intervention of Richard Ansdell, an indistinct figure who appears only occasionally, though following this Seth rises unaided to the editorship. Similarly, he is saved from committing adultery only because Albert returns home unexpectedly just as Seth is responding to Isabel's coquetry. Because of this he forfeits his moment of intended heroism; his intention of announcing his paper's opposition to Albert's corrupt candidacy shrivels in the heat of the husband's justified wrath: "You set yourself up to judge *me*; you arrogate to yourself airs of moral superiority, and assume to regulate affairs of State by the light of your virtue and wisdom — and you have not brains enough meanwhile to take care of yourself against the cheapest wiles of a silly woman, who amuses herself with young simpletons just to kill time." This humiliation disqualifies Seth as hero; his moral triumph is stillborn and he agrees to become Albert's political tool.

At this point Frederic's divided attitudes reach a fictional crisis. Is the democratic system capable of self-regulation through the virtues of its citizens and institutions, of frustrating the ambitions of the power-hungry who threaten to subvert it, or is the model Democratic Man naive and self-indulgent, powerless in his insufficiency? To put it another way, are the natural forces of probity capable of overcoming the forces of corruption, of evil, or are they themselves blighted by natural depravity? Seth, the instrument of Frederic's optimism, fatally disqualifies himself from action.

Yet Frederic is unwilling to accept the implications of Seth's failure. With the presumptive hero discredited, he moves outside of the social machinery he has created to salvage a positive resolution. A villain is made of an otherwise ineffectual farmhand, who preserves the integrity of the political process by murdering Albert, and an unexpected hero is made of a previously obscure third brother, John. John plays Fortinbras, reassembling the scattered plot pieces by occupying the farm which is the family patrimony and demonstrating an integrity as editor of his weekly newspaper which Seth could not sustain. Thus the "moral and spiritual laxity" are embodied in Seth, and the "honest and devoted leaders" are peripheral and dramatically neutral figures.

Frederic attempted to rectify the defects of *Seth* in the sequel, *The Lawton Girl* (1890). Following the apparent plan for the trilogy, he shifted his attention from politics to economics and treated urban problems. His working notes called for a single protagonist, but, warned by Seth's unreliability and not yet aware of the confusion of attitudes which Seth had embodied, he divided the original protagonist into two. Reuben Tracy receives all of Seth's admirable traits, while Horace Boyce receives his cupidity. Reuben is honest, sober, hard-working, and a bloodless prig; Horace is a self-deceiving lecher, a dilettante, a cheat, and at last a scoundrel. Yet it is Horace who wins the reader's interest and sympathy, again frustrating Frederic's intended optimism.

The story is built on two plot lines, Jessica Lawton's rehabilitation after her seduction by Horace and subsequent brothel degradation, and the rescue of the Minster Iron Works from a shadowy cartel, which, using Horace as an instrument, plans to seize it. With adequate materials for an energetic novel, *The Lawton Girl* nevertheless fails. Jessica's reclamation proceeds to the point of decent employment as a milliner, then founders on Frederic's unwillingness to allow her to marry the seducer she still loves. Furthermore, the economic bandits deserve more success in stealing the Minster factory than Frederic allows them. They are unconvincingly defeated in a dishonestly melodramatic climax: at the moment of crisis Reuben discovers documents which incriminate the gang, thereby earning him the hand and fortune of heiress Kate Minster.

"It was a false and cowardly thing to do," Frederic later wrote of his decision to kill Jessica rather than to allow her to marry Horace. But this self-criticism applies equally to his decision to employ twin protagonists. Reuben's perfection makes him incredible. He is qualified through natural gifts and unassailable character to restore community equilibrium, to the benefit of owner and worker alike, as the manless Minsters are not. In contrast, the selfishness and vanity of Horace are disruptive of the cosmic order and his every action threatens the communal well-being. Order and the "smiling" aspects of life triumph, but it is a triumph without dramatic validity. Reuben is never more than an animated fabrication, an artifact in the worst sense of the word, transmitted inert from Frederic's imagination to the printed page. Tellingly, most of the vitality emanates from the disreputable and unscrupulous figures. The dialogue, schemes, and actions of these figures are vital and fictionally engaging; those of their honest and decent counterparts are not. In a valid resolution of conflicts, order is not restored through the asceptic law-school oratory with which Reuben pacifies the rioting workers. As Frederic was writing, the meretriciousness of this climax was being demonstrated by riots in Chicago's Haymarket.

In 1890 Frederic also published his Revolutionary War romance, *In the Valley*. The appearance of a study of the origins of the nation at this time is suggestive. When the national character on which his "dramatic method" depended demonstrated moral instability, it was necessary to turn to the causative events which had produced that character, as Hart Crane and William Carlos Williams were later to do. Thus his impulses were epic, a search for cultural roots related to those of Homer, Virgil, and Camões, and it is as epic that Frederic's American historical fiction can most usefully be read.

In the Valley was actually completed sometime before *The Lawton Girl*, yet, with the Civil War tales which followed, it is a response to Frederic's philosophical and fictional dilemma. Frederic sought the symbols of the past which might explain the

present, and although *In the Valley* is scrupulously faithful to
historical and geographical fact, it is nevertheless the most completely symbolic of Frederic's works. Many of the characters represent factions of the Valley population: Douw Mauverensen, the
hero, the early European colonists; Philip Cross, his enemy, the
arrogant English aristocrats. Daisy, the girl of indeterminate ori-
gin, is a symbol of the land itself for which the two groups compete. Even the geography is symbolic: the Mohawk Valley which
divides the colonies culturally and strategically in two, and the
gorge which separates Douw's home from Philip's, both represent
the divisions between the settlers and between the Old World
and the New, which resulted in warfare and were healed at last
by brotherly reconciliation.

Its dimensions are epic as well. In time it reaches back through
the allusions and recollections of Douw to precolonial days, and
forward through its dramatic events, from 1757 to 1777, to the
time of narration, about 1815. Further, it is spatially immense,
sweeping from Europe (in the recalled background of Douw's pa-
tron) to the fur-trading encampments of the Midwest, and from
the early battles at Boston to the siege of Quebec. The cast of
characters is enormous, literally an army, a roll call of the German, Dutch, and English settlers whose differences and dogged-
ness precipitate and sustain the action. The events often corre-
spond with those of the traditional epic: the journey of the hero
into the wilderness to prepare him for his mature mission, the
premonitory vision given the hero of the final crucial battle, the
muster of the warriors, and the single combat between the hero
and his personal adversary within the larger framework of battle.

Frederic deftly navigates between the Scylla and Charybdis
which endanger the writer of historical fiction, the gratuitous introduction of famous men for fictional effect and the tendency to
sentimentalize or glorify the "forefathers." The hero is no pal-

adin, but a stubborn Dutchman whose occasional petulance humanizes him and prevents him from becoming a Reuben Tracy stereotype; although the villain is unpleasant, his arrogance and rascality result from the incompatibility of his aristocratic manners and assumptions with egalitarian frontier life. And Daisy comes to Douw not an immaculate virgin but the abused widow of his enemy, ravaged like the land by the struggle in which she is won.

America, Frederic concluded, is not simply a consequence of grafting an ideal system to a new unspoiled continent in which latter-day Adams and Eves started afresh under a new covenant. It is, in addition, a result of the melding of barely miscible ethnic elements on blood-tempered soil and the necessary catalyst is mutual tolerance. It is on this realistic foundation that the qualified promise of America stands. The implied danger, which tempts Douw, is that there may arise a new arrogance and intolerance which will invalidate the original victory. What is required, then, is manliness and unselfish responsibility which combine the best qualities of individualism with mutual understanding and respect between men. It is his inhumane treatment of a helpless slave which leads to the death of Philip Cross.

In the Valley is not wholly successful. Though the scenic elements and dramatic passages are technically excellent, the total effect is of events and places seen through a remote haze, and except for Douw the main characters seldom attain more than symbolic life. Frederic admitted that "their personalities always remained shadowy in my own mind." His style, elevated to meet the demands of an epic, loses force and stability in the process. Still, the novel is conceived with originality and deserves a prominent place in American historical fiction.

Following this Frederic traced the effects of independence during the period between Douw's growth to manly tolerance and

Seth Fairchild's reversion to paralyzing self-indulgence. At precisely what point had the national experiment failed, if it had, and what could be learned from the subsequent experiences which might illuminate and suggest remedies for the ills of the present? The Civil War had left vivid images of community apprehension and suffering on Frederic as a child, and to the maturing artist it attained a significance analogous to that of the War of Independence. Between these wars the nation had tested diverse political and social postures, had experienced waves of immigration, and, disturbingly, had begun to reorganize class distinctions. Great questions had remained unresolved: the relative supremacy of national and regional interests, and the willingness or unwillingness of individuals to suppress self-interest and tolerate divergent attitudes and ways in others.

The Copperhead (1893) begins at the point where *In the Valley* ended, tracing its protagonist's ideas back to the age of "Matty" Van Buren and to Jefferson. Opening on the outbreak of the war, it dramatizes the philosophical divisions which tore the nation, North and South alike. The copperhead (or sympathizer with the South) is Abner Beech, a states rights individualist who, though he does not support slavery, cannot accept self-righteous interference with southern affairs. His ideological opponent is an evangelical abolitionist named "Jee" Hagadorn. Their children are in love, a hopeful new generation capable of transcending the narrow attitudes which make enemies of their parents.

The theme of intolerance is repeated in *The Copperhead*. States rights and abolitionist attitudes lead to persecution rather than dialogue. Although he has been a farsighted "natural aristocrat" among the community farmers, Abner is now despised, banished from the cooperative dairy which he was instrumental in founding and deserted by his hired men. But Abner returns intolerance for intolerance: after his son joins the Union army, he reads the story of Absalom and David at family prayers and disinherits the boy. Mutual intolerance grows until, in an orgy of patriotic enthusiasm, his neighbors burn Abner's house unintentionally, to the horror of both sides. Local and national tragedy meet when Abner's son returns to the ashes of his home maimed by battle, and the implications of the formerly abstract dispute are made manifest in human suffering. Copperhead and abolitionist alike are chastened, and in a gesture of reconciliation the two children marry.

Marsena (1894 in serial form) anatomizes a form of seemingly innocent folly, the viciousness of which is revealed in the context of war, the egotism of a beautiful woman who gratifies herself by playing sexual roulette with human destiny. Marsena is an ironic self-portrait created in a tone lying somewhere between sharp self-criticism and tolerant whimsy. Affecting melancholy Byronic poses, he is impossibly romantic, as the young Frederic just returned from Boston may have been. His romanticism is soon focused on the aristocratic town flirt who is the ideal of the young men of the town, Julia Parmalee.

The comedy of the first scenes is rich as the gallants contest for Julia's attentions and as she lures them one by one into the militia as testimony of their devotion to her, dropping each at the conscript train. "If you only give her time, she'll have the whole male unmarried population of Octavius, between the ages of sixteen and sixty, down there wallerin' around in the Virginny swamps, feedin' the muskeeters and makin' a bid for glory," says the local philosopher. And that is exactly what happens when the comic-opera skirmishes of Lincoln's ninety-day army give way to the bitter struggle between heavily gunned opponents and all too real casualty lists begin to sum up the cost of Julia's flirtatious recruiting. The awkward chivalry of the town hopefuls and the mischievous arrogance of a town flirt take on a horrifying new significance in the vicious fighting; what begins as ironic comedy turns inexorably to bitter revulsion.

At this point the tone of an otherwise brilliant novella disintegrates. Perhaps lacking sufficient artistic detachment from its autobiographical protagonist, Frederic allows his outrage to take command. "It was one of the occasions on which Man had expended all his powers to prove his superiority to Nature. The elements in their wildest and most savage mood could never have wrought such butchery as this. . . . the broad, sloping hillside and the valley bottom lay literally hidden under ridge upon ridge of smashed and riddled human forms, and the heaped débris of human battle. The clouds hung thick and close above, as if to keep the stars from beholding this repellent sample of earth's titanic beast, Man, at his worst." Finally, in uncontrolled anger, Frederic provides an impossible ending, the callous Julia, now a socialite nurse at the front, ministering to a slightly scratched staff officer as Marsena dies clutching the hem of her skirt.

The epic cycle is concluded by "The War Widow" (1893), the last (in internal chronology) and the greatest of Frederic's historical fiction. It is a powerful novella which looks ahead from the tragedy of war into the coming Gilded Age to suggest, perhaps regretfully, a road not taken, the recapture from the experience of death and suffering of certain important human values.

Two living characters dominate the action along with two others about whom, though they are dead when the story begins, the action turns. Old Arphaxed Turnbull is an earthy Valley patriarch whose fathers cleared the land, made it say crops instead of briars, and built the prosperous farm which he has inherited and increased. Aunt Em, his daughter, is a taciturn, kindly woman, like her pioneer ancestors a vigorous household drudge without the slightest glamour, so plain that it is assumed that she will never marry. Nevertheless, one day she brings home a good-natured ne'er-do-well she has taken to husband. Although Abel Jones is hardly received as an ornament to the successful family, he is everything to Em. The fourth figure is Em's half-brother Alva, a brilliant, educated man whose early distinction promises fulfillment of Arphaxed's dynastic dreams; through Alva, Arphaxed glimpses a world of gentility he himself can never enter. When a local regiment is raised, it is natural that Alva ride away in command, sword at side, while Abel joins the rear rank as a private soldier.

The bereavement of war exposes Arphaxed's vanity: he has begun to revert to the repudiated European aristocratic ideals. His grief at the death of Alva is nearly unbearable, perhaps more because of the death of his dynastic ambitions than because of that of his son, while the death of Abel, though equally tragic, he ignores.

When Alva's casket is opened for a last time before he is to be buried in a hillside grave overlooking the Valley he might one day have ruled, Arphaxed is horrified to find that war profiteers have substituted the body of an anonymous enlisted man. The wives of the sons have experienced a real loss much greater than the frustration of Arphaxed's vision of family eminence, as have those who loved the soldier in the coffin. But in his unthinking rage Arphaxed orders the body sent to the county authorities for a pauper's burial. At this, Em angrily confronts her father. "On Resurrection Day, do you think them with shoulder-straps 'll be called fust an' given all the front places? I reckon the men that carried a musket are every whit as good, there in the trench, as them that wore swords. They gave their lives as much as the others did, an' the best man that ever stepped couldn't do no more." Chastened by Em's angry dignity and intimidated by the intercession of Alva's wife, Arphaxed buries the stranger in Alva's grave, in acknowledgment of the democracy of suffering of the living and the awful equality of the dead.

Frederic thus concluded that by the time of the Civil War there had been a rebirth of foreign vanities and illusions which the plain-featured and direct-spoken men and women of *In the Valley* had attempted to extirpate from the new democratic society, a rebirth which threatened corruption to the great ideal. However bigoted Abner Beech and Jee Hagadorn may have been, each still cherished individual human rights and unadorned virtues, and neither could have given Arphaxed's order to send away the symbolic coffin. Yet "The War Widow" suggests that amid the seemingly senseless slaughter and the unworthy ambitions of a newer kind of American, a rebirth of democratic brotherhood for the future American and an exorcism of the vanity which threatened to corrupt the "smiling" aspects of American life were possible.

That there had been a further transmission of Arphaxed's vanity to Seth Fairchild and Horace Boyce suggests that Frederic's suppressed fears would yet have to be accounted for. By the time of *Marsena*, the last published of the cycle, they had reached the surface, and the center of his Howellsian optimism was no longer able to hold. Death, the awful absolute which purges and chastens in "The War Widow," has by the time of *Marsena* lost its nobility, has become frivolous, a ghastly quean who scarcely notices as victims gasp at her feet. Vanity, not heroism, leads men to their deaths, and the society they die defending is not a community of dignified creatures but "earth's titanic beast, Man." Frederic saw that "an Egyptian blackness was over it all" in one of his last glances back over the American past.

In other ways aside from his shaken idealism 1890 was a watershed in Frederic's life, followed by a gradually increasing "Egyptian" darkness. The momentum of his success had begun to falter as early as 1887, when the baby Harold Frederic, who had been the focus of all his father's "hopes and aspirations," died. The following year his political hero, Cleveland, was denied re-election, challenging Frederic's faith that a democratic electorate would recognize integrity in its leaders. In addition, literary success proved elusive. Although critics like Howells praised *Seth* and fellow realists wrote their congratulations, the novel was foreign to the expectations of the mass of readers, who preferred their fiction perfumed with elegance, romance, and sentiment. It was alternately deplored and ignored by influential reviewers in the popular magazines and sales were poor. Far from achieving the financial independence which he was already anticipating in his standard of living, he was forced to continue indefinitely with the *Times*. He was settling into a nearly permanent pattern of high living and low sales which frustrated permanently his hope of abandoning the "fool-rink" of journalism for the life of a literary aristocrat.

He was still sanguine about *In the Valley*, however. Even if the public failed to respond to it, he expected a more favorable reaction from the perceptive few. But the most important of these failed him. Through an oversight, Howells had ignored Frederic completely until 1890, when, in a combined review of the first three novels, he buried praise for the others under condemnation of the intended masterpiece, calling it a "fresh instance of the fatuity of the historical novel." During a visit to Boston that year Frederic appealed his case in person and they parted on friendly terms. But Howells always remained aloof from Frederic and, for Frederic, Howells ceased to be the supreme trail-breaker and arbiter, though he always remained important as a leader in the search for literary truth.

In other areas Frederic experienced disappointments. In his favorite retreat, the Savage Club, a nasty quarrel broke out with a

London editor. Frederic was finally sued for libel, of which he was probably guilty. When he lost the suit, his estrangement from the Savages became permanent and this outlet for his ambitions and good spirits was closed. A similar catastrophe occurred in his relations with the Irish leaders. As a result of the scandal surrounding Parnell's marriage to the divorced Kitty O'Shea, Tim Healy contested his leadership. Frederic followed Healy's example, using his *Times* cable to repudiate the "lost leader." But Parnell's charisma with the Irish people remained and was abruptly transformed into martyrdom when he died tragically in 1891. Frederic found himself on the wrong side, a rational voice drowned in keening Irish emotionalism. He was never again influential among the Irish, and resentment against him ran high among the Irish in America. Whether for this reason or not, Frederic never returned to the United States.

Before 1890 Frederic hoped to attain eminence and affluence by marching to the Howells drum and conforming to the Horatio Alger Junior success pattern; thereafter he realized that he must create a compensating social and artistic world of his own. Increasingly, he sought out private friendships among writers and artists to substitute for the salon society of the Philistines, and aspired to success in the perfection of his artistry rather than in the reviewers' columns. Remarkable changes occurred beneath his hearty exterior, alterations in his ambitions, his loyalties, his habits, and, ultimately, his art. The bankrupt thrust toward public eminence was replaced by an ideal of inner growth and personal fulfillment.

It was in 1890 that Kate Lyon became his mistress. There was a certain idealism about the alliance, which accorded with his radical views of sexual relationships in the age of the New Woman. It was a genuine attempt to substitute a vital and joyous love for the hypocritical and sterile, though unseverable, bond which his marriage had become. There were both good and bad effects of the new liaison. He found purity in his relationship with Kate who, George Gissing claimed, was his "real wife"; she "saved him & enabled him to do admirable things." On the other hand, it may have been his heterodox love life that disqualified him from the Liverpool consulship, which, in a last effort to salvage his failing dream, he requested soon after Cleveland returned to the presidency in 1893.

Aside from his historical cycle, the years from 1890 to 1896 constitute a chaotic second "period" in Frederic's literary development. They were years filled with anguish and vexations, in which his adopted sociological realism was of little use to him, he had developed no substitute technique or philosophy, and the demands on his income were doubled by the needs of his two families. He was forced by poverty and aesthetic uncertainty to a broad range of literary experiments which produced some trivial work and some interesting results as well. Although this was a perplexing and uncomfortable time for him, it had one invaluable result. Along with the insights he was gaining into his own attitudes in his Civil War tales, the experience of dabbling in a variety of styles and subjects enabled him to perfect the craftsmanship which characterized the fiction of his last years.

This dabbling is imposing in its range. Infected with the theatrical fever which was endemic among his contemporaries Twain, Howells, and James, he worked both singly and in collaboration with Brandon Thomas (*Charley's Aunt*) on a number of plays. Few were completed, however, and of those which were only one was cast and rehearsed. He wrote journalistic books as well, an effective and influential study of contemporary anti-Semitism in Russia and a gossipy, unscholarly biography of the German Kaiser. In another vein, he wrote two inferior tales of the War of the Roses, which, though he attempted verisimilitude and historical accuracy, are unmistakably juvenile fiction. One further experiment, unsuccessful but suggestive of the direction which his later fiction would take, is the frankly Hawthornesque "The Song of the Swamp-Robin" (1891). Though Frederic misunderstood Hawthorne's genius and patterned the story after his worst rather than his best tales, it is significant that this early he was glancing away from the Howells imperatives toward the unfashionable moral romance.

There are two genuine achievements among these experiments, a social satire and a series of Irish tales. The first is a series of sketches of English middle-class society written for magazine publication in 1892 and collected as *Mrs. Albert Grundy: Observations in Philistia* (1896). Loosely linked by the scantest of courtship plots, they allowed Frederic to meander brightly and skillfully among whatever topics attracted him at the moment: self-portrait, character sketches, the English courts, middle-class prudery, and so forth. With deft control of tone he comments on matters as slight as the social consequences of shaving one's beard and as serious as the plight of a genteel woman thrown unprepared into the economic labyrinth of sexually unequal London. The style is nimble and urbane, the humor precise and delightfully understated; the reader coming to this book from the rough force of Frederic's early work is forced to reassess his versatility and recognize a finer sensibility than he is often said to have had. But there is a further dimension which underlies the surface delicacy. The sketches provided Frederic with an emotional release through which he could rid himself of some of the multiplying frustrations and disappointments of his daily life. Through the vertiginous Miss Timby-Hucks he was able to discharge his animosity toward women journalists, particularly a certain Miss Stevens who was employed by the *Times* to write feature letters about the Royal Academy art exhibitions despite Frederic's superior qualifications, and to strike back at the English courts following his conviction for libel. And in the reactions of the American outsider to English society he was enabled to comment on the British character and on the fate of being an American innocent confronted with old Europe.

It was natural that after Frederic's alienation from Irish affairs and after hope for Irish self-rule diminished he would turn to fiction to express his responses to the islanders whom he never ceased to love. After a false beginning with an abortive novel he produced an apparently uncompleted series of haunting tales of the O'Mahony septs, which, despite their small bulk, relate him to the Irish literary renaissance. The setting is his adopted area of southern Ireland, the Ivehagh peninsula, and the time is the last half of the sixteenth century, the period during which Ireland fell gradually under the domination of Elizabeth's generals. Alternately tragic and comic, they dramatize what Frederic conceived to be the salient qualities of the rich and contrary Irish character: bravery and treachery, seismic loves and hatreds, piety and superstition, and, pervading all, the fierce Irish pride. In execution they reveal Frederic at a new plateau of achievement, in full command of a supple style which ranges from lush lyricism to sparse tragedy.

There are four tales in all, begun and ended by stories concerned with the chieftainship of Turlogh of the Two Minds. He is an Irish Hamlet whose character, deficient in the passion and self-assertiveness which make other overlords feared warriors and unquestioned leaders, is reflective and gentle. He affords his kerns a wise rule which, if it disappoints their combative natures, echoes the great scholarly tradition of medieval Ireland and offers a hope, not to be realized in Turlogh's time, of a future of peaceful prosperity.

"In the Shadow of Gabriel" (1895) tells of the coming of age of

Turlogh, in which it is the studious youth rather than his terrified warriors who doggedly pursues the devil haunting his lands, and the "devil" who saves him from death at the hands of a supposed holy man. Through a topsy-turvy inversion of good and evil, wit and witlessness, bravery and cowardice, Turlogh wins the right to his fiefdom in a conclusion both comical and brutal. Ironic comedy is counterpointed in the second tale by the legendary tragedy of Murtogh and his unfaithful wife; the third returns to another coming-of-age rite, this one farcical, in which Teige, a boastful, lustful young chieftain, is gulled into a remarkably rewarding marriage by the lies of a cringing bard.

In the climaxing tale, "The Truce of the Bishop" (1895), the burial of a magnificently vain bishop is combined with the ritualistic death of Turlogh and his warriors in combat with the invading English. Turlogh is now an old man, his lands laid waste. The end of free Ireland is at hand; the only choice left to the now single-minded Turlogh is to submit or to perish on his own terms. Seizing control of the black fate of his sept, Turlogh conducts the bishop's last rites with all the magnificence left to him, then provokes a battle to the end with the astonished English. As he stands over their bodies, the English commander pronounces their epitaph: "Has ever there been such a land of madmen and saints?" He speaks as well for Frederic, who, looking back over the long history of Irish repression and self-destructiveness, was similarly perplexed by their heroic grandeur and suicidal passions.

At precisely this point Frederic's period of consolidation ended, his literary maturity complete. He had tested a broad spectrum of styles, subjects, and modes, and had refined his implements, rendering them responsive to subtle variations of thought and mood. He was, in addition, uniquely qualified for the important work ahead, the critical re-examination of the

Whitmanic democratic man. He had struggled to sustain his own faith, and when his optimism was suborned by the flawed character of his representative protagonists, he had probed the American past diagnostically, hoping in the process to discover some hope for future meliorization. But the heroism he discovered was confined to the remote past. As his fiction approached the present, he confronted the truth that men had not improved under egalitarian conditions; if anything, they had degenerated. Frederic's last measure of nineteenth-century optimism died on the battlefield with Marsena, clutching the skirts of a seductive ideal with which he had flirted.

Nor was this a purely literary discovery. In his rise from a modest background to international stature as a journalist, his life had approximated the American Dream. Yet for all of his high principles and dedication to the truth, his deepest impulses were undependable and self-defeating. His enemies could, after all, without departing wholly from the truth describe him as a gross man, a liar, a financial irresponsible, and an adulterer. As this self-knowledge grew, he sensed that the flaws of his protagonists were reflections of flaws within himself. He realized in the most personal way that the New World Adam was really post-lapsarian, his innocence confined to his manners and to his ideal conception of himself. Beneath was an uncharted subterranean cavern of id — or original sin, to vary the terminology — where obscene monsters might and too often did exist. As long as the innocence was imperfectly tested by experience, its surface might hold. But once it was shattered, the true nature of the democratic man was exposed.

Not even Henry James could perform this anatomization with his remarkably delicate scalpel; his imagination was confined to a social stratum above the Whitmanic quotidian and he was unable to deal with humdrum reality. Mark Twain had insufficient intellectual discipline and sense of form. Howells lacked brilliance of perception. Only Frederic could. His experience, his perception, his darkened vision, and his perfected talent made it possible. In his final phase of innocent-turned-cynic he asked himself inevitable questions. What was the fate of the American to be in the new, complex century about to arrive? And what was to be the fate of the world should its destiny fall into his hands? Frederic's answer was embodied in some of the most significant fiction of the era.

The Damnation of Theron Ware (1896) is a study of a new kind of American not-so-innocent, whose ancestors include both Huckleberry Finn and Faust. It is the story of a likable, talented, but ignorant young Methodist minister whose superficial religion and deficient character are challenged in the microcosmic Mohawk Valley city of Octavius. A teacup dilettante, he is thrust into a primitive parish to face a religious and cultural ugliness which he has heretofore been able to avoid. His good-natured weakness is inadequate to the challenge, and in revulsion he accepts offers of intellectual companionship from three figures whose philosophies offer sophisticated alternatives to the narrow fundamentalism of his parishioners: Father Forbes, a Catholic philosophical skeptic modeled on Father Terry; Doctor Ledsmar, an atheistic scientist; and, most attractive to Theron, Celia Madden, a beautiful and wealthy young woman who, though a Catholic, offers him aesthetic epicureanism. It is a classic instance of egocentric innocence confronted with the allure of exotic philosophies it fails to comprehend — indeed, is prevented from comprehending by an inherent voluptuousness concealed beneath a surface of affable charm. As Theron accepts their friendship, the terms of which he never bothers to ascertain, he turns his back on his parish, losing control over its affairs to the elders of the church. Just in time (for Theron's damnation) two pragmatic confidence men turned evangelists, Brother and Sister Soulsby, arrive for a "debt-raising." Taking his affairs into their hands, they reconcile minister and congregation. Thus the necessary forces are deployed for the paradigmatic loss of innocence of a tawdry American Adam. He must choose among them, and his choice leads to his damnation (the English edition of the book was ironically titled *Illumination*). But his fall is a peculiarly modern one, preordained by the conditions of the modern world, and reworked by Frederic into a pratfall into the twentieth century.

Theron Ware is one of the most widely misread novels in American literature, though in spite of Frederic's narrative subtlety and a certain ambiguity its meaning seems relatively clear. The conflicting values are those of his earlier fiction: goodheartedness and sincerity set against hypocrisy and self-seeking. Although the "European" triumvirate are occasionally associated with diabolical imagery (they have a diabolical *effect* on Theron) they are genuinely, if unwisely, anxious to help him rise to knowledge, each according to his own beliefs. Ledsmar lends him atheistic books, keeps reptiles, and experiments on the narcotics tolerance of his Chinese servant. Celia has flaming red hair and has converted her rooms to an exotic palace of pleasure where she promises to show Theron "that which is my very own." Forbes scoffs at literal interpretation of the scriptures, has ominously white skin and a plush, phallus-like body, and lives a sumptuously nonclerical life in the privacy of his pastorate. They must share some of the blame for destroying his innocence by their proselyting. Certainly they are careless, but each is genuinely concerned with his intellectual and spiritual growth. Such innocence as Theron's cannot endure in the modern world; how he reacts to their ministries is a function of his honesty.

The same cannot be said of Sister Soulsby, the true Mephi-

stopheles of the morality. Although through pure fictional vitality she is an engaging figure, she is a shape-changer, a disarmingly
frank and earthy woman who at the same time darts her eyes at
Theron like a bird of prey, advises him to have some of the "wisdom of the serpent," and bargains his church away from him
with a Faustian handshake. It is she who touches Theron's weak-
est point, immobilizing his moral faculties with a vision of petty illusions disguising the sordid "reality" of the world. "Did you
ever see a play? In a theatre, I mean. I supposed not. But you'll
understand when I say that the performance looks one way from
where the audience sit, and quite a different way when you are
behind the scenes. *There* you see that the trees and houses are
cloth, and the moon is tissue paper, and the flying fairy is a middle-aged woman strung up on a rope. . . . everything in this
world is produced by machinery — by organization."

With this "common sense" appeal she wins a permanent con-
vert to the cynical philosophy of sharp practices and self-indulgent rationalizations. Ware sees his ministry now as no more than
a theatrical illusion which he must stage-manage from the pulpit.
Father Forbes's traditional attacks on Protestant literalism he
now interprets as atheism and Celia's sincere commitment to
beauty he interprets as an invitation to petty vice. Ledsmar's
philosophical battles with Celia he supposes to be personally vindictive and he crudely attempts to use Ledsmar as an informant
against the other two. Under Sister Soulsby's pernicious tutelage
he believes that he is onstage where the machinery may be seen,
gaining every moment in moral stature and enlightenment, pene-
trating to the sordid motives behind human activity known only
to the favored few. But Celia's brother, with the insight of the
dying, knows better. "You are much changed, Mr. Ware, since
you came to Octavius, and it is not a change for the good. . . .
Only half a year has gone by, and you have another face on you

entirely . . . If it seemed to me like the face of a saint before, it is more like the face of a bar-keeper now!"

In technique the novel is Hawthornesque, except for Frederic's deceptively realistic prose. Most of the proper names are heavily allusive and the passage of the seasons symbolizes a reversal of the regeneration of *Walden*. It moves from emblem to emblem, embodying meaning in those still-life pictures which have been characteristic of classic American fiction from its beginnings — Leatherstocking silhouetted against the sky, Dimmesdale standing bare-chested on a Boston scaffold, Bulkington glimpsed frozen to the *Pequod's* tiller. The decay of the modern ministry is displayed in the hierarchical arrangement of the assembly of the Methodist Conference; Theron's revulsion from the fundamentalists and his attraction to the sophisticates are repeated in his reactions to the squalor of his parsonage yard and the lush foliage next door; the foreign allure of Celia's paganized Christianity is reflected in the decor of her apartment; and Theron's youthful prejudice against Catholics is remembered in a Nast-like cartoon of sinister priests.

When Theron meets Celia in a remote wood, halfway between the austere frenzy of a Methodist camp meeting and the Dionysian revelry of a Catholic picnic, they discover the novel's central emblem. "The path they followed had grown indefinite among the grass and creepers of the forest carpet; now it seemed to end altogether in a little copse of young birches, the delicately graceful stems of which were clustered about a parent stump, long since decayed and overgrown with lichens and layers of thick moss." The path lost and the solid beliefs of the past rotted away, tentative alternatives compete for dominance, though none now dominates. Theron is free to choose, but his choice must be sincere, positive, creative, rather than nihilistic. Above all, he must recognize that the new shoots are real and alive, not, as Sister

Soulsby insists, illusory. When he does not, his damnation is assured.

Furthermore, it is a damnation against which Frederic himself struggled. For the qualities which animate the central characters are fractions of his own complex personality. Within, the same alternatives were at war: the hopeful, opportunistic Theron is the young reporter arriving in London; the Darwinian horticulturalist Ledsmar is Frederic; the epicurean Celia is Frederic; and the glib charlatan Sister Soulsby is Frederic. Alice Ware, the simple wife abandoned by the upward-seeking Theron is Grace Frederic, that tragic woman left behind in isolation and bitterness by her ambitious husband. The city of Octavius is more than a microcosm of innocent America at last confronting the complexities of Europe and the coming century; it is an allegory of the spirit of a diverse and troubled man who fatally senses the centrifugal drama being enacted within him.

Whatever doubts he may have had about his own character, Frederic had none about Theron's. When he elects Sister Soulsby's bad faith, the rest is downward spiral. Succumbing to the logic of his degeneration, he becomes successively a would-be adulterer, an embezzler, a Peeping Tom, and a near murderer and suicide before returning to Sister Soulsby, now her creature. Not recognizing his new allegiance to the Prince of Darkness, he claims that God has forsaken him. Alice, more empirical, claims that "it was all that miserable, contemptible Octavius that did the mischief." But Sister Soulsby, who should know, replies that "if there hadn't been a screw loose somewhere . . . Octavius wouldn't have hurt him." At the end Theron is stuffed with straw and set on his feet again, now ambitious for the one career which, since Albert Fairchild, has always meant damnation in Frederic's fiction: seeking political power for his own profit and for the satisfaction of his damaged ego.

Theron Ware is a powerful masterpiece. It presents not only a brilliantly conceived and psychologically fascinating protagonist but a representative if unpromising man at the end of an era of confidence and simple faith and the beginning of a darker era of complexity and doubt. It is only from the perspective of the present that we can see the full significance of what Frederic discerned at the end of the nineteenth century. The era to come — our era — would demand an inner strength much greater than had been required of men before. Deprived of the comforting assurances of the past, the modern man would be forced back upon the resources of his own character, his virtues, to use a nearly outmoded term, in order to make his way among the tangle of often questionable choices of the world-maze. To look for stage machinery instead of truth is to invite degeneration, to confuse darkness with illumination, to strike a bargain with Satan, to lose what weed-grown Paradise is left in a diminished world.

Frederic's own slight version of Paradise, the solace he found in his mistress Kate Lyon, is the subject of a small, graceful novel written in reaction to the darkness of *Theron Ware*. Perhaps beauty in this world *is* stage illusion. In that case, a temporary stay against despair may be had by preserving the illusion. *March Hares* (1896) is the story of such protective self-deception, of failure and emptiness eluded by an escape into an artificial fairyland, embraced and substituted for distasteful truth.

The story opens on the September reality of London. David Mosscrop, a brilliant time-server in a meaningless sinecure, has wasted his life in stale dissipation with oafish companions, and stands on Westminster Bridge, unshaven, groggy with drink, contemplating suicide. There he meets a despondent young woman who, without money or friends, also considers suicide or prostitution. What follows was known as "cat-fiction" at the time. The two band together, fall in love, and on David's modest resources command that September dissolve and that the freshness of March return. They eat and drink, buy new clothes, disappear and reappear, and finally, in a minuet of mistaken identities, are reunited. The reality of September is only precariously suppressed, awaiting a moment of depression or misunderstanding to reassert itself, but as long as both agree to the mutual enchantment it is March.

Perhaps his life with Kate was necessary to save Frederic from destruction, as the story suggests. Nevertheless, the novel is unfulfilled, ending in irresolution. The basic failure of David's life, his wasted brilliance and the meaningless squirrel-cage of his profession, is in the end unchanged. It is disguised but present, to reappear again when the illusion of March can no longer be sustained. Kate Lyon may have been a defense against despair, but in story and life alike the fates remained unplacated behind the make-believe of happiness.

With the popular success of *Theron Ware*, Frederic at last gained acceptance as a man of letters, though on far different terms from the Bostonian dignity he had sought. He was in demand as a reviewer, accepted in important intellectual circles, and acquainted with Shaw, Gissing, James, Conrad, Wells, and Ford Madox Ford. Yet it was with a fellow American journalist that he had his only intimate literary association. Stephen Crane, who praised his Civil War fiction and was praised by him in turn, met Frederic in London on his way to the war in Greece, and on his return moved into a suburban house Frederic had secured. The two novelists and their mistresses were companions, frequenting each other's homes and vacationing together in Ireland. The relationship was occasionally stormy, and the two added little or nothing to each other's art. Nevertheless, it was the kind of alliance Frederic had long sought to substitute for the neglects and disappointments of his later life, and he threw himself into it with enthusiasm.

But the idyl ended when Crane departed abruptly for the Spanish-American War. Frederic's heart was failing just when his intellectual and artistic powers were at their peak. Doctors were called, but with fatalistic independence he lived his last days on his own terms, refusing all advice and care. As his body declined he punished it contemptuously, driving furiously across the country, smoking cigars, and drinking. When this was no longer possible, Kate sent for a Christian Science healer, and the two women attempted to substitute faith for the medicine he refused. On October 19, 1898, Frederic died, leaving a heavy legacy of debt and recrimination to his two families. A vindictive trial followed, in which Kate and the healer were spared imprisonment only because of a judicial determination that, despite Frederic's difficult personality, he was sane at the time of his illness and capable of seeking medical aid had he desired it. Thus the man who aspired to dignified eminence ended his life in the midst of scandal and vituperation.

Following the trial, Frederic's two posthumous novels enjoyed wide circulation among the curious. It was a surprise to his readers and a disappointment to reviewers to find that both were set in England. The subject matter, paralleling in many ways that of *Seth* and *The Lawton Girl*, makes it appear that he had in mind another trilogy, this one "studying" English life. That this was the case is strongly suggested by the combined historical allegory and political-sociological didacticism of *Gloria Mundi* (1898), an unfortunately artificial and weak novel. It yokes a shadowy recapitulation of the origins and development of the English people to a yet-unraveled *roman à clef* of contemporary English society. In the peregrinations of the French-born protagonist, whose prospective inheritance of an impoverished English barony provides the primary plot thread, the book wanders over a lot of territory, solves no problems, and ends in irresolution.

The novel suggests that the cosmic order exists as Frederic had earlier supposed, but now indifferent to men, who can no longer prosper by harmonizing with it. After considering the various uses to which he may put his titled prerogatives, Christian Tower decides at the end that it is useless to adopt any program at all. His dukedom is "all a great organized machine, like some big business." "A man is only a man after all. He did not make this world, and he cannot do with it what he likes. It is a bigger thing, when you come to think of it, than he is. At the end there is only a little hole in it for him to be buried in and forgotten." Perhaps a premonition of Frederic's death can be read into this passage. If so, Christian's stoicism contrasts sharply with the vision of immortality which had been before Frederic in Albany fifteen years earlier.

Frederic returned to the force of *Theron Ware* in his remarkable last novel, *The Market-Place* (1899). In a sinewy narrative he utilizes the world of London finance to develop the central theme of his last years, the implications of the chaotic century which was about to arrive for the directionless people who must live in it. For this purpose he unleashed a selfish, brutal speculator (developed from Sister Soulsby) named Joel Stormont Thorpe on a decayed society which, seeking a hero, invites a dictator. Representative figures of the mordant English ruling class surround him: a marquis of ancient family, a newer aristocrat, a retired general, all impecunious and prepared to sacrifice principle for cash. The degeneracy of these atrophied remains of traditional European authority is manifest; the question raised is, after them what?

The inevitable answer is that with the erosion of the hereditary estates of rule, the power vacuum will be filled with or without the intelligent assent of the governed. To the illuminated, troubled author the future seemed clouded and ambiguous, potential leaders grasping and amoral, and the citizenry apathetic. Power seemed within the reach of greedy, arrogant men, and this danger was amplified by the seeming sanction given to the domineering ego by some of the more alarming implications of the philosophies of Carlyle and Nietzsche. Good and evil, they suggested to some readers, at least, are defined by the whims of the new aristocrat, the barbarian whose lust for power and efficiency in gaining it provide a new pragmatic standard of conduct. If this were true, then it invalidated Frederic's remaining belief in the commonwealth of humanity; if it were false, then the very currency of the concept lent an appearance of respectability to demagoguery, social vandalism, and megalomania.

While literary naturalists assented to the new philosophy, Frederic offered an example whose strength, will, and amorality approximate those of the superman, but who is at the same time human, originating within the social structure rather than above it. Thorpe is fallible, lacking the ability to crush his victims at will. In dozens of earlier escapades this middle-aged fortune hunter has been balked by bad luck, traitorous associates, or perhaps his own bungling. It is only in his present stock-market swindle that circumstances combine to allow him success, and now only because of the arrogant miscalculations of the financiers who oppose him.

With success, Thorpe demonstrates prophetically the implications of Nietzsche's abstractions when twisted to suit the purposes of the demagogue. His swindle assumes an anti-Semitic character; boasting of his power, he says, " 'I used to watch those Jews' hands, a year ago, when I was dining and wining them. They're all thin and wiry and full of veins. Their fingers are never still; they twist round and keep stirring like a lobster's feelers. But there aint any real strength in 'em. They get hold of most things that are going, because they're eternally on the move. It's their hellish industry and activity that gives them such a pull, and makes most people afraid of them. But when a hand like that takes them by the throat' — he held up his right hand as he spoke, with the thick uncouth fingers and massive thumb arched menacingly in a powerful muscular tension — 'when *that* tightens round their neck, and they feel that the grip means business — my God! what good are they?' He laughed contemptuously." His pillage becomes murderous when an old derelict endangers his scheme and is quietly eliminated in a final solution. Thorpe's appearance changes into that of an Adolf Hitler, as he trims his mustache to military size and becomes jowly. "It was palpably the visage of a dictator."

Thorpe's scheme prospers, partly because his greed is shared by his victims, and partly because of the exhaustion of the moral resources of decency. Both are embodied in the woman he marries. There is an element of masochistic sexual aberration in Edith Cressage, whose blood has run thin and whose normal responsiveness has been vitiated by her marriage to a degenerate aristocrat, forced upon her by her corrupt father. Now she is willing to submit to Thorpe's crude force, seeing in it a stimulant to her exhausted feminine appetites and a mastery to which she can sublimate her disappointed need for personal fulfillment.

After Thorpe has made his fortune, married, and retired to a country manor, the final warning is given. He is dissatisfied with the opulent life which had earlier been his goal, for there is no satisfaction for the power-seeker except in the pursuit of power. Therefore, in a much-misread ending, Thorpe returns to London to spend his money charitably among the poor — except that his largess will be bartered for a seat in Parliament, and ultimately for power over all England. One of the judges who voted to behead Charles I was a Thorpe, he reminds us.

Frederic's deft manipulation of point of view makes severe demands on the reader's discrimination; one must be attentive to his road markers. Tension builds as the financial scheme alternates between apparent success and the constant danger of collapse, and as Thorpe's courtship is alternately frustrated and successful. The temptation to sympathize with an energetic figure who is also a scoundrel makes Thorpe's success all the more insidious. Evil appearing as evil is dangerous; evil masquerading as gumption, individualism, shrewdness, the American Dream, is a transcendent danger which can only be evaluated by the most exacting attention to humane principle. That is precisely Frederic's point. It is only by listening to the voice of principle, here that of Celia Madden (carried over from *Theron Ware*) and Thorpe's sister, that gross misreadings of the novel, such as attributing Thorpe's anti-Semitism to Frederic, can be avoided. There are numerous other pitfalls for the unwary, such as believing Thorpe's self-characterization at the end as a new man with new ideas. There is no new, humanized Thorpe; he is still a "man gathering within himself, to expend upon his fellows, the appetites, energies, insensibilities, audacities of a beast of prey." He is a twentieth-century political pirate, seizing power with stolen money. Celia's last analysis of him is accurate. "I shall always insist . . . that crime was his true vocation."

Recognition came to Frederic late, and then for the wrong reasons. *Theron Ware* was read because of its scandalous impiety; *The Market-Place* because of the scandal surrounding his death. Soon thereafter, interest in his work subsided, and he has been a victim of the "effacing march of generations" which he dreaded. To a certain extent this neglect has been justified. Beginning with a journalistic conception of literature, and lacking Henry

James's ability to theorize about the nature of fiction and to translate theory into practice, Frederic tended on occasion to write dramatized essays rather than novels. Not only that, but he was curiously inept with essay materials and in these novels he was often betrayed by the unresolved conflict between his ideology and the dramatic reality which embodied most faithfully his deepest understanding of the nature of men. It was only in his last three years that this conflict was resolved and his mature genius found expression. When it did, his achievement was too far in advance of current attitudes to be comprehensible to his public.

Nor has subsequent criticism been notably perceptive. Readers have classified him as a regionalist, as a realist, and as a naturalist, whereas his true descent from Hawthorne and Melville has largely gone unnoticed. Many sense the depth and power of *Theron Ware*, but find the source of his creative energy elusive.

Frederic's achievement lies in the sensitivity and power with which he probed the naiveté and inconsistency of the American Dream and announced its inevitable collapse in the face of the new order of complexity of the twentieth century. In this he surpassed all his contemporaries in his ability to dramatize, allegorize, and mythicize the coming fall from innocence. In addition, testing his vision against his own experience, he understood that a loss of innocence might not bring a dignified, saddened wisdom, but might transform youthful egotism into debased cynicism, and ultimately into predatory rapacity. Thus Frederic wrote for the twentieth century, not his own, and in his greatest works achieved a vigorous and alarming vision of the civilization to come which has, as we can now see, verified his worst fears and proved him to be one of the most perceptive and important novelists of his time.

◢ Selected Bibliography

Principal Works of Harold Frederic

NOVELS

Seth's Brother's Wife: A Study of Life in the Greater New York. New York: Scribner's, 1887.

In the Valley. New York: Scribner's, 1890.

The Lawton Girl. New York: Scribner's, 1890.

The Return of the O'Mahony. New York: Bonner's, 1892.

The Copperhead. New York: Scribner's, 1893.

Mrs. Albert Grundy: Observations in Philistia. London: Lane, 1896.

The Damnation of Theron Ware. Chicago: Stone and Kimball, 1896. Published in England with a few textual variations as *Illumination.* London: Heinemann, 1896.

March Hares. London: Lane, 1896. Initially issued under the pseudonym "George Forth."

Marsena. London: Unwin, 1896. (Serialized in 1894.)

Gloria Mundi: A Novel. Chicago and New York: Stone, 1898.

The Market-Place. New York: Stokes, 1899.

COLLECTIONS OF FICTION

The Copperhead and Other Stories of the North during the American War. London: Heinemann, 1894. (Contains "My Aunt Susan," *The Copperhead,* "The Eve of the Fourth," and "The War Widow.")

Marsena and Other Stories of the Wartime. New York: Scribner's, 1894. (Contains "My Aunt Susan," "The Eve of the Fourth," "The War Widow," and *Marsena.*)

In the Sixties. New York: Scribner's, 1897. (Contains a preface which is Frederic's only systematic discussion of his work, as well as all of the fiction in the preceding two items.)

The Deserter and Other Stories: A Book of Two Wars. Boston: Lothrop, 1898. (Contains "Where Avon into Severn Flows," "How Dickon Came by His Name," "The Deserter," and "A Day in the Wilderness.")

MAJOR UNCOLLECTED SHORT STORIES

"Brother Angelan," *Harper's*, 73:517–28 (September 1886).

"The Editor and the Schoolma'am," *New York Times*, September 9, 1888, p. 14.

"The Martyrdom of Maev," *New York Ledger*, 46:1–3 (March 22, 1890), and 46:1–3 (March 29, 1890).

"The Song of the Swamp-Robin," *Independent*, 43:394–95, 430–32 (March 12 and 19, 1891).

"Cordelia and the Moon," *Liber Scriptorum*. New York: Author's Club, 1893 Pp. 241–52.

"The Path of Murtogh," *Idler* (London), 7:455–79 (May 1895).

"The Truce of the Bishop," *Yellow Book*, 7:84–111 (October 1895).

"In the Shadow of Gabriel. A.D. 1550," *New York Ledger*, 51:12–13 (December 21, 1895); *Black and White*, 10:21–26 (Christmas 1895).

"The Wooing of Teige," *Pall Mall Magazine*, 10:418–26 (November 1896).

"The Connoisseur," *Saturday Review* (London), 82:18–21 (Christmas 1896); *New York Ledger*, 52:8–9 (January 2, 1897).

NONFICTION BOOKS

The Young Emperor, William II of Germany: A Study in Character Development on a Throne. New York: Putnam's, 1891.

The New Exodus: A Study of Israel in Russia. New York: Putnam's, 1892.

CURRENT AMERICAN REPRINT

The Damnation of Theron Ware. Cambridge, Mass.: Harvard University Press. $1.65. New York: Holt, Rinehart and Winston. $1.50.

Bibliography

American Literary Realism, 1870–1910, 2:1–89 (Spring 1968). (Secondary and some primary bibliography.)

Blanck, Jacob. *Bibliography of American Literature*, III. New Haven, Conn.: Yale University Press, 1959.

Woodward, Robert H. "Harold Frederic: A Bibliography," *Studies in Bibliography*, 13:247–57 (1960).

Biographical and Critical Studies

Berryman, John. *Stephen Crane*. New York: Sloane, 1950.

Carter, Everett. "Introduction," *The Damnation of Theron Ware*. Cambridge, Mass.: Harvard University Press, 1960.

Crane, Stephen. "Harold Frederic," *Chap-Book*, 8:358–59 (March 15, 1898).

Earnest, Ernest. *Expatriates and Patriots*. Durham, N.C.: Duke University Press, 1968.

Garner, Stanton. "Some Notes on Harold Frederic in Ireland," *American Literature*, 39:60–74 (March 1967).

Gilkes, Lillian. *Cora Crane: A Biography of Mrs. Stephen Crane*. Bloomington: Indiana University Press, 1960.

Haines, Paul. "Harold Frederic." Ph.D. dissertation, New York University, 1945. (Still the standard biography.)

Johnson, George W. "Harold Frederic's Young Goodman Ware: The Ambiguities of a Realistic Romance," *Modern Fiction Studies*, 8:361–74 (Winter 1962–63).

Kane, Patricia. "Lest Darkness Come upon You: An Interpretation of *The Damnation of Theron Ware*," *Iowa English Yearbook*, 10:55–59 (Fall 1965).

Lovett, Robert Morss. "Introduction," *The Damnation of Theron Ware*. New York: Boni, 1924.

McWilliams, Carey. "Harold Frederic: 'A Country Boy of Genius,' " *University of California Chronicle*, 35:21–34 (1933).

O'Donnell, Thomas F. "Editor's Foreword," *Harold Frederic's Stories of York State*. Syracuse: Syracuse University Press, 1966.

————, and Hoyt C. Franchere. *Harold Frederic*. New York: Twayne, 1961. (A fundamental study, with information not in Haines.)

Raleigh, John Henry. "*The Damnation of Theron Ware*," *American Literature*, 30:210–27 (May 1958).

Ravitz, Abe C. "Harold Frederic's Venerable Copperhead," *New York History*, 41:35–48 (January 1960).

Towers, Tom H. "The Problem of Determinism in Frederic's First Novel," *College English*, 26:361–66 (February 1965).

Walcutt, Charles Child. *American Literary Naturalism, a Divided Stream*. Minneapolis: University of Minnesota Press, 1956.

Wilson, Edmund. "Introduction," *Harold Frederic's Stories of York State*. Syracuse: Syracuse University Press, 1966.

Woodward, Robert H. "The Political Background of Harold Frederic's Novel *Seth's Brother's Wife*," *New York History*, 43:239–48 (July 1962).

————, "Some Sources for Harold Frederic's *The Damnation of Theron Ware*," *American Literature*, 32:46–51 (March 1961).

Ziff, Larzer. *The American 1890's; Life and Times of a Lost Generation*. New York: Viking, 1966.